WEATHER
Clouds

by Ann Herriges

BELLWETHER MEDIA • MINNEAPOLIS, MN

Note to Librarians, Teachers, and Parents:

Blastoff! Readers are carefully developed by literacy experts and combine standards-based content with developmentally appropriate text.

Level 1 provides the most support through repetition of high-frequency words, light text, predictable sentence patterns, and strong visual support.

Level 2 offers early readers a bit more challenge through varied simple sentences, increased text load, and less repetition of high-frequency words.

Level 3 advances early-fluent readers toward fluency through increased text and concept load, less reliance on visuals, longer sentences, and more literary language.

Whichever book is right for your reader, Blastoff! Readers are the perfect books to build confidence and encourage a love of reading that will last a lifetime!

This edition first published in 2007 by Bellwether Media.

Library of Congress Cataloging-in-Publication Data
Herriges, Ann.
  Clouds / by Ann Herriges.
    p. cm. — (Blastoff! readers) (Weather)
Summary: "Simple text and supportive images introduce beginning readers to the characteristics of clouds. Intended for students in kindergarten through third grade."
  Includes bibliographical references and index.
  ISBN-10: 1-60014-024-6 (hardcover : alk. paper)
  ISBN-13: 978-1-60014-024-2 (hardcover : alk. paper)
  1. Clouds—Juvenile literature. 2. Weather—Juvenile literature. I. Title. II. Series.
  QC921.35.H47 2007
  551.57'6–dc22
                                    2006000615

Text copyright © 2007 by Bellwether Media.
Printed in the United States of America.

Table of Contents

Clouds float across the sky.
Clouds are made of
water drops.

Some clouds are made
of ice **crystals**.

Clouds form when warm air rises and cools. The colder air cannot hold as much water as the warm air. Some of the water changes into tiny drops.

The water drops mix with **dust** in the air. The water drops and dust clump together to make clouds.

Clouds carry water to the earth. Rain falls from clouds when the air is warm.

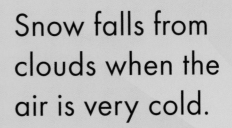

Snow falls from clouds when the air is very cold.

Clouds come in many shapes and sizes.

Some clouds are high in the sky.
Some clouds are low in the sky.

Cirrus clouds are curly and wispy. Sometimes they look like a horse's tail.

Cirrus clouds are thin enough
to see through. Stormy weather
could be coming if cirrus clouds
are in the sky.

Cumulus clouds look like cotton balls. They are puffy on top and flat on the bottom. Cumulus clouds that are small and white bring good weather.

Sometimes cumulus clouds grow bigger and taller. They become dark **cumulonimbus** clouds. These clouds bring thunderstorms.

Stratus clouds are low in the sky. They are flat and can be thick or thin.

Rain or snow can fall
from stratus clouds.
Sometimes the rain
is light **drizzle**.

A cloud close to the ground is **fog**. Fog forms when the earth is warm and the air is cool and **moist**.

Sometimes wind blows fog away. Sometimes fog dries up in the heat of the sun.

Meteorologists study the weather. The shapes of the clouds tell them what kind of weather is coming next.

Look up in the sky. What kind of weather do you see in the clouds?

Glossary

cirrus—thin, wispy clouds that form high in the sky

crystal—a solid that has a pattern of many flat sides; an ice crystal is water frozen into a six-sided solid.

cumulonimbus—tall, white clouds that are flat and dark on the bottom; cumulonimbus clouds bring thunderstorms with heavy rain and lightning.

cumulus—clouds that are flat on the bottom and puffy on top; cumulus clouds form low in the sky.

drizzle—a light, misty rain

dust—tiny bits of matter floating in the air; tiny water drops stick to soil, sea salt, and other dust to form clouds.

fog—a cloud close to the ground

meteorologist—someone who studies the weather

moist—a little wet

stratus—flat, gray clouds that often cover the sky

To Learn More

AT THE LIBRARY

Bauer, Marion Dane. *Clouds*. New York: Aladdin, 2004.

De Paola, Tomie. *The Cloud Book*. New York: Holiday House, 1984.

Gibbons, Gail. *Weather Words and What They Mean*. New York: Holiday House, 1990.

Greene, Carol. *Hi, Clouds*. Chicago: Children's Press, 1983.

Walker, Rob D. *Once Upon a Cloud*. New York: Blue Sky Press, 2005.

ON THE WEB
Learning more about the weather is as easy as 1, 2, 3.

1. Go to www.factsurfer.com

2. Enter "weather" into search box.

3. Click the "Surf" button and you will see a list of related web sites.

With factsurfer.com, finding more information is just a click away.

Index

The photographs in this book are reproduced through the courtesy of: Photodisc, front cover; Johner/Getty Images, p. 4; Werran/Ochsner/Getty Images, p. 5; National Geographic Society/Getty Images, pp. 6, 8-9; Mary Clay/Getty Images, p. 7; Rob Atkins /Getty Images, p. 9; Luc Beziat/Getty Images, p. 10; Tom Bean/Getty Images, p. 11; Naoki Okamoto/Getty Images, p. 12; Darryl Torckler/Getty Images, p. 13; Joseph Van Os/Getty Images, p. 14; Mike Magnuson/Getty Images, p. 15; Aurora/Getty Images, pp. 16-17; Stephen Krasemann/Getty Images, p. 17; Gary Randall/Getty Images, pp. 18-19; 2003 Getty Images, p. 20; Michael Smith/Getty Images, p. 21.